How to Write a Play

Various

Contents

INTRODUCTION 7
I. From Emile Augier. 14
II. From Theodore de Banville. 16
III. From Adolphe Dennery. 18
IV. From Alexandre Dumas Fils. 19
V. From Edmond Gondinet. 23
VI. FROM Eugene Labiche. 25
VII. From Ernest Legouve. 27
VIII. From Edouard Pailleron. 30
IX. From Victorien Sardou. 35
X. From Emile Zola. 37
NOTES 39

HOW TO WRITE A PLAY

BY

Various

INTRODUCTION

The impression has always prevailed with me that one who might properly be classed as a genius is not precisely the person best fitted to expound rules and methods for the carrying on of his particular branch of endeavor. I have rather avoided looking the matter up for fear it might not turn out to be so after all. But doesn't it sound as if it ought to be? And isn't a superficial glance about rather confirmatory? We do not--so far as I know--find that Shakspere or Milton or Tennyson or Whitman ever gave out rules and regulations for the writing of poetry; that Michael Angelo or Raphael was addicted to formulating instructive matter as to the accomplishment of paintings and frescoes; that Thackeray or Dickens or Meredith or George Sand were known to have answered inquiries as to 'How to write a Novel'; or that Beethoven or Wagner or Chopin or Mendelsohn paused in the midst of their careers in order to tell newspaper men what they considered the true method of composing music. These fortunate people--as well as others of their time--could so easily be silent and thus avoid disclosing the fact that they could not--for the lives of them--tell about these things; but in our unhappy day even geniuses are prodded and teased and tortured into speech. In this case we may be more than grateful that they are, for the result is most delightful reading--even tho it falls a trifle short of its purpose as indicated by the rather far-reaching title.

There are no workable rules for play-writing to be found here--nor, indeed, any particular light of any kind on the subject, so the letters may be approacht with a mind arranged for enjoyment. I would be sorry indeed for the trying-to-be dramatist who flew to this volume for consolation and guidance. I'm sorry for him any way, but this additional catastrophe would accelerate my sympathy, making it fast and furious. Any one sufficiently inexperienced to consult books in order to find out how to write a play will certainly undergo a severe touch of confusion in this case, for four of the letter-writers confess quite frankly that they do not know--two of these thereupon proceeding to tell us, thus forcibly illustrating their first statement. One author exclaims, "Have instinct!"--another, "Have genius!" Where these two necessaries are to be obtained is not revealed. Equally discouraging is the Dumas declaration that "Some from birth know how to write a play and the others do not and never will." That would have killed off a lot of us--if we had seen it in time.

One approaches the practical when he counsels us to "Take an interesting theme." Certainly a workable proposition. Many dramatists have done that--wherever they could find it. The method is not altogether modern. Two insist upon the necessity of a carefully considered plan, while two others announce that it is a matter of no consequence what one does; and another still wants us to be sure and begin work at the end instead of the beginning. Gondinet--most delightful of all--tells us that his method of working is simply atrocious, for all he asks when he contemplates writing a play is whether the subject will be amusing to him. Tho that scarcely touches the question of how to write it, it is a practical hint on favoring conditions, for no one will dispute that one's best work is likely to be preformed when he him self enjoys it. Sardou comes nearest to projecting a faint ray of practical light on the subject when he avers that there is no one necessary way to write a play, but that a dramatist must know where he is going and take the best road that leads there. He omits, however, to give instructions about finding that road--which some might think important.

The foregoing indicates to some extent the buffeting about which a searcher for practical advice on play-writing may find himself subject in this collection of letters. He had better go for mere instruction to those of a lower order of intellect, whose imaginative or creative faculties do not monopolize their entire mental area.

But that will hardly serve him better, for the truth is that no one can convey to him--whether by written words or orally--or even by signs and miracles--the right and proper method of constructing a play. A few people know, but they are utterly unable to communicate that knowledge to others. In one place and one only can this unfortunate person team how to proceed, and that is the theatre; and the people to see about it there are situated in front of the foot-lights and not behind them.

A play or drama is not a simple and straight-told story; it is a device--an invention--a carefully adjusted series of more or less ingenious traps, independent yet inter-dependent, and so arranged that while yet trapping they carry forward the plot or theme without a break. These traps of scene, of situation, of climax, of acts and tableaux or of whatever they are, require to be set and adjusted with the utmost nicety and skill so that they will spring at the precise instant and in the precise manner to seize and hold the admiration--sympathy--interest--or whatever they may be intended to capture, of an audience. Their construction and adjustment--once one of the simplest--is now of necessity most complicated and intricate. They must operate precisely and effectively, otherwise the play--no matter how admirable its basic idea--no matter how well the author knows life and humanity, will fail of its appeal and be worthless--for a play is worthless that is unable to provide itself with people to play *to*. The admiration of a few librarians on account of certain arrangements of the words and phrases which it may contain can give it no value as drama. Such enthusiasm is not altogether unlike what a barber might feel over the exquisite way in which the hair has been aranges on a corpse; despite his approval it becomes quite necessary to bury it.

The play-writer's or playwright's work, then, supposing that he possesses the requisite knowledge of life as it is lived to go on with, is to select or evolve from that knowledge the basic idea, plot or theme, which, skillfully displayed, will attract; and then to invent, plan, devise, and construct the trap wherein it is to be used to snare the sympathies, etc., of audiences.

But audiences are a most undependable and unusual species of game. From time immemorial their tastes, requirements, habits, appetites, sentiments and general characteristics have undergone constant change and modification; and thus continues without pause to the present day. The dramatic trap that would work like a charm not long ago may not work at all to-day; the successful trap of to-day may be useless junk tomorrow.

It must be obvious, then, that for light and instruction on the judicious selection of the bait, and on the best method or methods of devising the trap wherein that bait is to be displayed (that is to say the play) but one thing can avail; and that one thing is a most diligent and constant study of the habits and tastes of this game which it is our business to capture--if we can. To go for information about these things to people sitting by their firesides dreaming of bygone days, or, indeed, to go to anyone sitting anywhere, is merely humorous. The information which the dramatist seeks cannot be told--even by those who know. For the gaining of such knowledge is the acquirement of an instinct which enables its possessor automatically to make use of the effective in play-writing and construction and devising, and automatically to shun the ineffective. This instinct must be planted and nourisht by more or less (more if possible) *living* with audiences, until it becomes a part of the system--yet constantly alert for the necessary modifications which correspond to the changes which the tastes and requirements of these audiences undergo.

An education like this is likely to take the dramatist a great deal of time--unless he is so fortunate as to be a genius. Perhaps the main difference between the play-writing genius and the rest of us is that he can associate but briefly with audiences and know it all, whereas we must spend our lives at it and know but little. I have never happened to hear of a genius of this description; but that is no argument against the possibility of his existence.

As to the talented authors of these letters, they know excellently well--every one of them--how to write a play--or did while still alive--even tho some of them see fit to deny it; but they cannot tell *us* how to do it for the very good reason that it cannot be told. Their charming efforts to find a way out when cornered by such an inquiry as appears to have been made to them are surely worth all their trouble and annoyance--not to speak of their highly probable exasperation.

                                      William Gillette (May, 1916)

                *   *   *   *   *

I.
From Emile Augier.

My dear Dreyfus:

You ask me the recipe for making comedies. I don't know it; but I suppose it should resemble somewhat the one given by the sergeant to the conscript for making cannon:

"You take a hole and you pour bronze around it."

If this is not the only recipe, it is at least the one most followed. Perhaps there should be another which would consist in taking bronze and making a hole thru the center and an opening for light at the end. In cannon this hole is called the core. What should it be called in dramatic work? Find another name, if you don't like that one.

These are the only directions I can give you. Add to them, if you wish, this counsel of a wise man to a dramatist in a difficulty:

"Soak your fifth act in gentle tears, and salt the other four with dashes of wit."

I do not think that the author followed this advice.
Cordially yours,
E. Augier

II.
From Theodore de Banville.

My dear friend:

Like all questions, the question of the theater is infinitely more simple than is imagined. All poetics, all dramatic criticism is contained in the admirable dictum of Adolphe Dennery: "It is not hard to succeed in the theater, but it is extremely hard to gain success there with a fine play."

To see this clearly you must consider two questions which have no relation to each other:

1. How should one set about composing a dramatic work which shall succeed and make money?

2. How shall one set about composing a dramatic work which shall be fine and shall have some hope of survival?

Reply to the first question: Nothing is known about it; for if anything were known every theater would earn six thousand francs every evening. Nevertheless, a play has some chance of succeeding and earning money if, when read to a naif person, it moves him, amuses him, makes him laugh or weep; if it falls into the hands of actors who play it in the proper spirit; and if at the public performance the leader of the *claque* sees no hitch in it.

Reply to the second question: To compose a dramatic work which shall be fine and shall live, have genius! There is no other way. In art talent is nothing. Genius alone lives. A poet of genius combines in himself all poets past and future, just as the first person you meet combines in himself all humanity past and present. A man of genius will create for his theater a form which has not existed before him and which after him will suit no one else.

That, my friend, is all that I know, and I believe that anything further is a delusion. Those who are called "men of the theater" (that is, in plain words, unlettered men who have not studied anywhere but on the stage) have decreed that a man knows the theater when he composes comedies according to the particular formula invented by M. Scribe. You might as well say that humanity began and ended with M. Scribe, that it is he who ate the apple with Eve and who wrote the 'Legendes des Siecles,' Good Luck!

                Yours truly,
                Theodore de Banville

III.
From Adolphe Dennery.

    Take an interesting theme, a subject neither too new nor too old, neither too commonplace or too original,--so as to avoid shocking either the vulgar-minded or the delicate-souled.
                                      Adolphe Dennery.

IV.
From Alexandre Dumas Fils.

My dear fellow-craftsman and friend:

You ask me how a play is written. You honor me greatly, but you also greatly embarrass me.

With study, work, patience, memory, energy, a man can gain a reputation as a painter, or a sculptor, or a musician. In those arts there are material and mechanical procedures that he can make his own, thanks to ability, and can attain to success. The public to whom these works are submitted, having none of the technical knowledge involved, from the beginning regard the makers of these works as their superiors: They feel that the artist can always reply to any criticism: "Have you learned painting, sculpture, music? No? Then don't talk so vainly. You cannot judge. You must be of the craft to understand the beauties," and so on. It is thus that the good-natured public is frequently imposed on, in painting, in sculpture, in music, by certain schools and celebrities. It does not dare to protest. But with regard to drama and comedy the situation is altered. The public is an interested party to the proceedings and appears, so to speak, for the prosecution in the case.

The language that we use in our play is the language used by the spectators every day; the sentiments that we depict are theirs; the persons whom we set to acting are the spectators themselves in instantly recognized passions and familiar situations. No preparatory studies are necessary; no initiation in a studio or school is indispensable; eyes to see, ears to hear--that's all they need. The moment we depart, I will not say from the truth, but from what they think is truth, they stop listening. For in the theater, as in life, of which the theater is the reflexion, there are two kinds of truth; first, the absolute truth, which always in the end prevails, and secondly, if not the false, at least the superficial truth, which consists of customs, manners, social conventions; the uncompromising truth which revolts, and the pliant truth which yields to human weakness; in short, the truth of Alceste and that of Philinte.

It is only by making every kind of concession to the second that we can succeed in ending with the first. The spectators, like all sovereigns--like kings, nations, and women--do not like to be told the truth, all the truth. Let me add quickly that they have an excuse, which is that they do not know the truth;--they have rarely been told it. They therefore wish to be flattered, pitied, consoled, taken away from their preoccupations and their worries, which are nearly all due to ignorance, but which they consider the greatest and most unmerited to be found anywhere, because their own.

This is not all; by a curious optical effect, the spectators always see themselves in the personages who are good, tender, generous, heroic whom we place on the boards; and in the personages who are vicious or ridiculous they never see anyone but their neighbors. How can you expect then that the truth we tell them can do them any good?

But I see that I am not answering your question at all.

You ask me to tell you how a play is made, and I tell you, or rather I try to tell you, what must be put into it.

Well, my dear friend, if you want me to be quite frank, I'll own up that I don't know how to write a play. One day a long time ago, when I was scarcely out of school, I asked my father the same question. He answered: "It's very simple; the first act clear, the last act short, and all the acts interesting."

The recipe is in reality very simple. The only thing that is needed in addition is to know how to carry it out. There the difficulty begins. The man to whom this recipe is given is somewhat like the cat that has found a nut. He turns it in every direction with his paw because he hears something moving in the shell--but he can't open it. In other words, there are those whom from their birth know how to write a play (I do not say that the gift is hereditary); and there are those who do not know at once--and these will never know. You are a dramatist, or you are not; neither will-power nor work has anything to do with it. The gift is indispensable. I think that every one whom you may ask how to write a play will reply, if he really can write one, that he doesn't know how it is done. It is a little as if you were to ask Romeo what he did to fall in love with Juliet and to make her love him; he would reply that he did not know, that it simply happened.

     Truly yours,
     A. Dumas *fils*.

V.
From Edmond Gondinet.

My dear friend:
What is my way of working? It is deplorable. Do not recommend it to any one. When the idea for a play occurs to me, I never ask myself whether it will be possible to make a masterpiece out of it; I ask whether the subject will be amusing to treat. A little pleasure in this life tempts me a great deal more than a bust, even of marble, after I am gone. With such sentiments one never accomplishes anything great.

Besides, I have the capital defect for a man of the theater of never being able to beat it into my head that the public will be interested in the marriage of Arthur and Colombe; and nevertheless that is the key to the whole situation. You simply must suppose the public a trifle naif,--and be so yourself.

I should be so willingly, but I can't bring myself to admit that others are.

For a long time I imagined that the details, if they were

ingenious, would please the public as much as an intrigue of which the ultimate result is usually given in the first scene. I was absolutely wrong, and I have suffered for it more than once. But at my age one doesn't reform. When I have drawn up the plan, I no longer want to write the piece. You see that I am a detestable collaborator. Say so, if you speak to me, but don't hold me up as a model.

      Edmond Gondinet.

VI.
FROM Eugene Labiche.

Everyone writes in accordance with his inspiration and his temperament. Some sing a gay note, others find more pleasure in making people weep.

As for me, this is my procedure:

When I have no idea, I gnaw my nails and invoke the aid of Providence.

When I have an idea, I still invoke the aid of Providence,--but with less fervor, because I think I can get along without it.

It is quite human, but quite ungrateful.

I have then an idea, or I think I have one.

I take a quire of white paper, linen paper--on any other kind I can imagine nothing--and I write on the first page:

PLAN.

By the plan I mean the developed succession, scene by scene, of the whole piece, from the beginning to the end.

So long as one has not reached the end of his play he has neither the beginning nor the middle. This part of the work is obviously the most laborious. It is the creation, the parturition.

As soon as my plan is complete, I go over it and ask concerning each scene its purpose, whether it prepares for or develops a character or situation, and then whether it advances the action. A play is a thousand-legged creature which must keep on going. If it slows up, the public yawns; if it stops, the public hisses.

To write a sprightly play you must have a good digestion. Sprightliness resides in the stomach.

Eugene Labiche.

VII.
From Ernest Legouve.

You ask me how a play is made.

By beginning at the end.

A novel is quite a different matter.

Walter Scott, the great Walter Scott, sat down of a morning at his study-table, took six sheets of paper and wrote 'Chapter One,' without knowing anything else about his story than the first chapter. He set forth his characters, he indicated the situation; then situation and characters got out of the affair as best they could. They were left to create themselves by the logic of events.

Eugene Sue often told me that it was impossible for him to draw up a plan. It benumbed him. His imagination needed the shock of the unforeseen; to surprize the public he had to be surprized himself. More than once at the end of an instalment of one of his serial stories he left his characters in an inextricable situation of which he himself did not know the outcome.

George Sand frequently started a novel on the strength of a phrase, a thought, a page, a landscape. It was not she who guided her pen, but her pen which guided her. She started out with the intention of writing one volume and she wrote ten. She might intend to write ten and she wrote only one. She dreamed of a happy ending, and then she concluded with a suicide.

But never have Scribe, or Dumas *pere*, or Dumas *fils*, or Augier, or Labiche, or Sardou, written "Scene One" without knowing what they were going to put into the last scene. A point of departure was for them nothing but an interrogation point. "Where are you going to lead me?" they would ask it; and they would accept it only if it led them to a final point, or to the central point which determined all the stages of the route, including the first.

The novel is a journey in a carriage. You make stops, you spend a night at the inn, you get out to look at the country, you turn aside to take breakfast in some charming spot. What difference does it make to you as a traveler? You are in no hurry. Your object is not to arrive anywhere, but to find amusement while on the road. Your true goal is the trip itself.

A play is a railway journey by an express train--forty miles an hour, and from time to time ten minutes stop for the intermissions; and if the locomotive ceases rushing and hissing you hiss.

All this does not mean that there are no dramatic masterpieces which do not run so fast or that there was not an author of great talent, Moliere, who often brought about his ending by the grace of God. Only, let me add that to secure absolution for the last act of 'Tartuffe' you must have written the first four.

Ernest Legouve.

VIII.
From Edouard Pailleron.

You ask me how a play is made, my dear Dreyfus. I may well astonish you, perhaps, but on my soul and honor, before God and man, I assure to you that I know nothing about it, that you know nothing, that nobody knows anything, and that the author of a play knows less about it than any one else.

You don't believe me?

Let us see.

Here is a capable gentleman, a man of the theater, a dramatist acclaimed a score of times, at the height of his powers, in full success. He has written a comedy. He has bestowed upon it all his care, all his time, all his ability. He has left nothing to chance.

He has just finisht it, and is content. According to the consecrated expression, it is "certain to go." But as he is cautious, he does not rely entirely upon his own opinion. He consults his friends--fellow-workers, skillful as he, successful as he. He reads to them his piece. I will not say that they are satisfied-

-another word is needed--but at any rate, with more reason than ever, it is "certain to go."

He seeks out a manager, an old stager who has every opportunity for being clear-headed, because of his experience, and every reason for being exacting, because of his self-interest. He gives him the manuscript, and as soon as the manager gets a fair notion of the piece, this Napoleon of the stage, this strategist of success, is seized by a profound emotion, but one easy to comprehend in the case of a man who is convinced that five hundred thousand francs have just been placed in his hand. He exults, he shouts, he presses the author in his arms, he rains upon him the most flattering adjectives, beginning with "sublime" and mounting upward. He calls him the most honied names: Shakspere, Duvert and Lauzanne, Rossini, Offenbach--according to the kind of theater he directs. He is not only satisfied, he is delighted, he is radiant--it is "certain to go."

Wait! That is not all. It is read to the actors--the same enthusiasm! All are satisfied, if not with the play--they have not heard it yet--at least with their parts. All are satisfied! It is "certain to go."

Thereupon rehearsals are held for two months before those who have the freedom of the theater, who sit successively in the depths of the dark hall and show the same delirium. Even the sixty firemen on duty who, during these sixty rehearsals, have invariably laught and wept at the same passages. Yet it is well known that the fireman is the modern Laforet of our modern Molieres, as M. Prud'homme would say, and that when the fireman is satisfied--it is "certain to go!"

The dress rehearsal arrives. A triumph! Bravos! Encores! Shouts! Recalls! All of the signs of success--and note that the public on this evening of rehearsal with the exception of a small and insignificant contingent, will be the public of the first performance the next night. It is "certain to go," I tell you! Certain! Absolutely certain!

On this next night the piece is presented. It falls flat! Well, then?

If the author knows what he is doing, if he is the master of his method, explain to me then why, after having written twenty good pieces, he writes a bad one?

And don't tell me that failure proves nothing--you would pain me, my friend.

I do not intend to deny, you must understand, the value of talent and skill and experience. They are, philosophically speaking, important elements. But in what proportions do they contribute to the result? That's what, let me repeat, nobody knows, the author as little as anybody else.

The author in travail with a play is an unconscious being, whatever he may think about himself; and his piece is the product of instinct rather than of intention.

Believe me, my dear Dreyfus, in this as in everything, the

cleverest of us does what he can, and if he succeeds, he says that he has done exactly what he tried to do. That's the truth. In reality an author knows sometimes what he has tried to do, rarely what he has done;--and as to knowing how he did it, I defy him!

Then if it is good, let him try again! I cannot recede from this view.

In our craft, you see, there is an element of unrebeginnable which makes it an art, something of genius which ennobles it, something of the fatally uncertain which renders it both charming and redoubtable. To try to pick the masterpiece to pieces, to unscrew the ideal, to pluck the heart out of the mystery, after the fashion of the baby who looks for the little insect in the watch, is to attempt a vain and puerile thing.

Ah! if I had the time--but I haven't the time. So it's just as well, or better, that I stop. To talk too much about art is not a good sign in an artist. It is like a lover's talking too much about love; if I were a woman I should have my doubts.

Well, do you wish me to disengage the philosophy of this garrulity? It is found whole and entire in an apolog of my son--he too a philosopher without knowing it. He was then seven. As a result of learning fables he was seized with the ambition of writing one, which he brought to me one fine day. It is called the 'Donkey and the Canary.' The verses are perhaps a trifle long, but there are only two. That's the compensation. Here they are.

The canary once sang; and the ass askt him how he could learn this to do?

"I open my bill," said the bird; "and I say you, you, you!"

Well, the ass, that's you--don't get angry. The canary, that's I. When I sing I open my bill and I say, "you, you, you!"

That's all that I can tell you.

Edouard Pailleron.

IX.
From Victorien Sardou.

My dear friend:
It's not so easy to answer you as you think. ...There is no one necessary way of writing a play for the theater. Everyone has his own, according to his temperament, his type of intellect, and his habits of work. If you ask me for mine, I should tell you that it is not so easy to formulate as the recipe for duck *a la rouennaise* or spring chicken *au gros sel*. Not fifty lines are needed, but two or three hundred, and even then I should have told you only my way of working, which has no general significance and makes no pretense to being the best. It's natural with *me*, that's all. Besides, you will find it indicated in part in the preface to 'La Haine' and in a letter which I wrote to La Pommeraye about 'Fedora.'

In brief, my dear friend, tho there are rules, and rules that are invariable, precise, and eternal for the dramatic art, rules which only the impotent, the ignorant, blockheads, and fools misunderstand, and from which only they wish to be freed, yet there is only one true method for the conception and parturition of a play--which is, to know quite exactly where you are going and to take the best road that leads there. However, some walk, others ride in a carriage, some go by train, X hobbles along, Hugo sails in a balloon. Some drop behind on the way, others run past the goal. This one rolls in the ditch, that one wanders along a cross-road.

In short, that one goes straight to the mark who has the most common sense. It is the gift which I wish for you--and myself also.

Victorien Sardou.

X.
From Emile Zola.

My dear Comrade:

You ask how I write my plays. Alas! I should rather tell you how I do not write them.

Have you noticed the small number of new writers who take their chances in the theater? The explanation is that in reality, for our generation of free artists, the theater is repugnant, with its cookery, its hobbles, its demand for immediate and brutal success, its army of collaborators, to which one must submit, from the imposing leading man down to the prompter. How much more independent are we in the novel! And that's why, when the glamor of the footlights makes the blood dance, we prefer to exercise it by keeping aloof and to remain the absolute masters of our works. In the theater we are asked to submit to too much.

Let me add that in my own case I have harnessed myself to a group of novels which will take twenty-five years of my life. The theater is a dissipation which I shall doubtless not permit myself until I am very old.

After all, if I could indulge in the theater. I should try to *make* plays much less than is the custom. In literature truth is always in inverse proportion to the construction. I mean this: The comedies of Moliere are sometimes of a structure hardly adequate, while those of Scribe are often Parisian articles of marvellous manufacture.

Very cordially yours,
Emile Zola.

NOTES

ABRAHAM DREYFUS (1847-) was the author of half a dozen ingenious little plays, mostly confined to a single act. One of them, 'Un Crane sans un Tempete,' adapted into English as the 'Silent System,' was acted in New York by Coquelin and Agnes Booth. Dreyfus was also the author of two volumes of lively sketches lightly satirizing different aspects of the French stage,--'Scenes de la vie de theatre' (1880) and 'L'Incendie des Folies-Plastiques' (1886).

In the Spring of 1884 he delivered an address on the art of playmaking before the Cercle Artistique et Litteraire of Brussels. This lecture was entitled 'Comment se fait une piece de theatre;' and it was printed privately in an edition limited to fifty copies, (Paris: A. Quantin, 1884). In the course of this address he read letters received by him from ten or twelve of the most distinguisht dramatists of France in response to his request for information as to their methods of composition. It was to these letters that the lecture owed its interest and its value. What M. Dreyfus contributed himself was little more than a running commentary on the correspondence that he had collected. This commentary was characteristically clever, brisk, bright and amusing; but its interest was partly personal, partly local, and partly contemporary. The interest of the letters themselves is permanent; and this is the reason why it has seemed advisable to select the most significant of them and to present them here unincumbered by the less useful remarks of the lecturer.

Emile Augier (1820-1889) disputes with Alexandre Dumas the foremost place among the French dramatists of the second half of the nineteenth century. The 'Gendre de M. Poirier' (which he wrote in collaboration with Jules Sandeau) is the masterpiece of modern comedy, a worthy successor to the 'Tartuffe' of Moliere and the 'Marriage of Figaro' of Beaumarchais.

Theodore de Banville (1823-1891) was a poet rather than a playwright. Altho he composed half-a-dozen little pieces in verse, the only one of his dramatic efforts which really succeeded in establishing itself on the stage, was 'Gringoire,' a one-act comedy in prose; and this met with a more fortunate fate than its more fantastic companions only because Banville revised and strengthened his plot in accordance with the skilful suggestions of Coquelin, who "created" the part of the starving poet.

Adolphe Dennery (1811-1899) was the most adroit and fertile of melodramatists in the midyears of the nineteenth century. Perhaps his best play was 'Don Cesar de Bazan'; and perhaps his most popular play was the 'Two Orphans.'

Alexandre Dumas *fils* (1824-1895) was the son of the author of the 'Three Guardsmen'; and he inherited from his father the native gift of playmaking, which he declared in this letter to be the indispensable qualification of the successful dramatist. His 'Dame aux Camelias' has held the stage for more than sixty years and has been performed hundreds of times in every modern language.

Edmond Gondinet (1828-1888) was the author of a host of pleasant pieces, mostly comedies in from one to three acts, and mostly written in collaboration. He believed that he preferred to write alone and that only his good nature kept tempting him into working with others. It was probably to warn away those who wanted to bring him their manuscripts for expert revision that led him to assert in this letter that he was "a detestable collaborator."

Ernest Legouve (1807-1903) was the collaborator of Scribe in the composition of 'Bataille de Dames' and 'Adrienne Lecouvreur.' In his delightful recollections, 'Soixante Ans de Souvenirs' he has a chapter on Scribe in which he describes the methods of that master-craftsman in dramatic construction; and in one of his 'Conferences Parisiennes' he sets forth the successive steps by which another dramatist, Bouilly, was able to compound his pathetic piece, the 'Abbe de l'Epee';--two papers which deserve careful study by all who wish to apprehend the principles of playmaking.

Eugene Labiche (1815-1888) was the most prolific of the comic dramatists of France in the nineteenth century and the most richly endowed with comic force. Most of his pieces are frankly farcical, but not a few of them rise to the level of true comedy. The solid merit of his best work is cordially recognized in the luminous preface written by Augier for the complete collection of Labiche's comedies.

Edouard Pailleron (1834-1899) was a comic dramatist of more aspiration than inspiration; and yet he succeeded in writing one of the most popular pieces of his time;--the 'Monde ou l'on s'ennuie.'

Victorien Sardou (1831-1908) was probably the French playwright who was most widely known outside of France. In the course of fifty years he was successful in almost every kind of playwriting, from lively farce to historic drama. His first indisputable triumph was with 'Pattes de Mouche,' known in English as the 'Scrap of Paper' and as widely popular in our language as in the original.

Emile Zola (1840-1902) was a novelist who repeatedly sought for success as a dramatist, attaining it only in the adaptations of his stories made by professional playwrights. Yet one of his earlier pieces, 'Therese Raquin' is evidence that he might have mastered the art of the playwright, if he had not allowed himself to be misled by his own unfortunate theory of the theatre as set forth in his severe studies of 'Nos Auteurs Dramatiques' (1881).

In the 'Annee Psychologique' for 1894 the distinguisht physiological psychologist, the late Alfred Binet,--to whom we are indebted for the useful Binet tests--publisht a series of papers dealing with the psychology of the playwright, in the preparation of which he was aided by M.J. Passy. The two investigators had a series of interviews with Sardou, Dumas *fils*, Pailleron, Meilhac, Daudet, and Edmond de Goncourt. Altho Daudet and Goncourt had written plays they were essentially novelists with no instinctive understanding of the drama as a specific art. Nor did either Pailleron and Meilhac make any contribution of importance. But Dumas and Sardou were both of them born playwrights of keen intelligence, having a definite understanding of the principles of playmaking; and what they said to M. Binet and his associate was interesting and significant.

Dumas declared that he made no notes for any of his plays and that he never composed a detailed scenario. He thought of only one piece at a time, brooding over it for long months sometimes, and then throwing it on paper almost at white heat, if it dealt with passion. If, on the other hand, it was a comedy of character, a study of social conditions, the actual composition was necessarily more leisurely and protracted. He had carried in mind for six or seven years the theme of 'Monsieur Alphonse;' and he had actually put it on paper in seventeen days. He had written the 'Princesse Georges' in three weeks and the 'Etrangere' in a month; and the second act of the 'Dame aux Camelias' had been penned in a single session of four hours. But he had toiled seven or eight hours a day for eleven months over the 'Demi-Monde,' the second act alone costing him two months labor. He rarely modified what he had written by minor corrections; but sometimes, when his play was completed, he discovered that it was weak in its structure or inadequate in its motivation, in which case he reconstructed one or more acts, or even the whole play, writing it all over again.

M. Dumas admitted that he took little interest in the setting of his plays or in the manifold details of stage-management. He indicated summarily the kind of room that he desired; and he put down in his manuscript only the absolutely necessary movements of his characters. The rest he left to the manager and the stage-manager.

Here--as indeed everywhere,--Dumas revealed himself in the sharpest contrast with Sardou, who designed his sets himself and placed his furniture precisely where he needed it for the action of his play, sometimes finding that a given scene seemed to him to lose half its effect if it was acted on the left side of the stage instead of the right. He was a constant note-taker, putting down suggestions for single scenes or for striking suggestions, as these might occur to him; and as a result of this incessant cerebral activity he had always on hand more or less complete plots for at least fifty plays. When he decided to write one of these pieces, he assembled his scattered notes, set them in order, amplified and strengthened them; and when at last he saw his way clear he made out an elaborate and detailed scenario, containing the whole story, with ample indication of all the changes of feeling which might take place in any of the characters in any scene.

Then when he felt himself in the right mood, he feverishly improvized the play, laughing over the jokes, weeping over the pathetic moments and objurgating the evil deeds of the more despicable characters. But this was only a first draft of the play; and it had to be gone over three or four times, altered, condensed, sharpened, tightened in effect. The first version was always too long; and the successive revisions reduced it to scarcely more than a half of its original length. Sometimes he was able to compact into a single pregnant phrase the substance of a speech of many lines. And as the play slowly took on its final form Sardou not only heard every word which every character had to speak, he also saw every one of the movements which would animate the action. M. Binet reminded him that when Scribe and Legouve were collaborating on 'Adrienne Lecouvreur,' Scribe asserted that he visualized all that the actors would do, while Legouve heard all that they would say; and Sardou then claimed that he was fortunate in possessing the double faculty of both seeing and hearing.

Of course, Sardou stage-managed his plays himself, teaching the performers carefully, and going upon the stage, if need be, to act the scene as he wanted it to be acted, indicating the expression, the intonation and the gesture which he felt to be demanded by the situation.

He was equally meticulous in designing the scenery and the costumes; and he was inexorable in insisting on the carrying out of his wishes. He had a lively interest in painting, in sculpture and in architecture; and, in fact, he confest, that if he had not been a playwright he would like to have been an architect. This, it may be noted, is conformation of the statement that there is a strong similarity between the art of architecture and the art of the drama, due to the fact that both arts are under the necessity of providing a solid structure to sustain the fabric and to support the decoration.

B.M.

www.bookjungle.com *email: sales@bookjungle.com fax: 630-214-0564 mail: Book Jungle PO Box 2226 Champaign, IL 61825*

The Codes Of Hammurabi And Moses
W. W. Davies

QTY

The discovery of the Hammurabi Code is one of the greatest achievements of archaeology, and is of paramount interest, not only to the student of the Bible, but also to all those interested in ancient history...

Religion   **ISBN: *1-59462-338-4***   **Pages:132**
MSRP $12.95

The Theory of Moral Sentiments
Adam Smith

QTY

This work from 1749. contains original theories of conscience amd moral judgment and it is the foundation for systemof morals.

Philosophy   **ISBN: *1-59462-777-0***   **Pages:536**
MSRP $19.95

Jessica's First Prayer
Hesba Stretton

QTY

In a screened and secluded corner of one of the many railway-bridges which span the streets of London there could be seen a few years ago, from five o'clock every morning until half past eight, a tidily set-out coffee-stall, consisting of a trestle and board, upon which stood two large tin cans, with a small fire of charcoal burning under each so as to keep the coffee boiling during the early hours of the morning when the work-people were thronging into the city on their way to their daily toil...

Childrens   **ISBN: *1-59462-373-2***   **Pages:84**
MSRP $9.95

My Life and Work
Henry Ford

QTY

Henry Ford revolutionized the world with his implementation of mass production for the Model T automobile. Gain valuable business insight into his life and work with his own auto-biography... "We have only started on our development of our country we have not as yet, with all our talk of wonderful progress, done more than scratch the surface. The progress has been wonderful enough but..."

Biographies/   **ISBN: *1-59462-198-5***   **Pages:300**
MSRP $21.95

www.bookjungle.com email: sales@bookjungle.com fax: 630-214-0564 mail: Book Jungle PO Box 2226 Champaign, IL 61825

The Art of Cross-Examination
Francis Wellman

QTY

I presume it is the experience of every author, after his first book is published upon an important subject, to be almost overwhelmed with a wealth of ideas and illustrations which could readily have been included in his book, and which to his own mind, at least, seem to make a second edition inevitable. Such certainly was the case with me; and when the first edition had reached its sixth impression in five months, I rejoiced to learn that it seemed to my publishers that the book had met with a sufficiently favorable reception to justify a second and considerably enlarged edition. ...

Reference   ISBN: *1-59462-647-2*   **Pages:412** MSRP *$19.95*

On the Duty of Civil Disobedience
Henry David Thoreau

QTY

Thoreau wrote his famous essay, On the Duty of Civil Disobedience, as a protest against an unjust but popular war and the immoral but popular institution of slave-owning. He did more than write—he declined to pay his taxes, and was hauled off to gaol in consequence. Who can say how much this refusal of his hastened the end of the war and of slavery?

Law   ISBN: *1-59462-747-9*   **Pages:48** MSRP *$7.45*

Dream Psychology Psychoanalysis for Beginners
Sigmund Freud

QTY

Sigmund Freud, born Sigismund Schlomo Freud (May 6, 1856 - September 23, 1939), was a Jewish-Austrian neurologist and psychiatrist who co-founded the psychoanalytic school of psychology. Freud is best known for his theories of the unconscious mind, especially involving the mechanism of repression; his redefinition of sexual desire as mobile and directed towards a wide variety of objects; and his therapeutic techniques, especially his understanding of transference in the therapeutic relationship and the presumed value of dreams as sources of insight into unconscious desires.

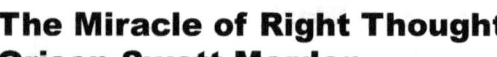

Psychology   ISBN: *1-59462-905-6*   **Pages:196** MSRP *$15.45*

The Miracle of Right Thought
Orison Swett Marden

QTY

Believe with all of your heart that you will do what you were made to do. When the mind has once formed the habit of holding cheerful, happy, prosperous pictures, it will not be easy to form the opposite habit. It does not matter how improbable or how far away this realization may see, or how dark the prospects may be, if we visualize them as best we can, as vividly as possible, hold tenaciously to them and vigorously struggle to attain them, they will gradually become actualized, realized in the life. But a desire, a longing without endeavor, a yearning abandoned or held indifferently will vanish without realization.

Self Help   ISBN: *1-59462-644-8*   **Pages:360** MSRP *$25.45*

www.bookjungle.com email: sales@bookjungle.com fax: 630-214-0564 mail: Book Jungle PO Box 2226 Champaign, IL 61825

QTY

	Title	ISBN	Price
☐	**The Rosicrucian Cosmo-Conception Mystic Christianity** by *Max Heindel*	ISBN: *1-59462-188-8*	**$38.95**
	The Rosicrucian Cosmo-conception is not dogmatic, neither does it appeal to any other authority than the reason of the student. It is: not controversial, but is: sent forth in the, hope that it may help to clear...		New Age/Religion Pages 646
☐	**Abandonment To Divine Providence** by *Jean-Pierre de Caussade*	ISBN: *1-59462-228-0*	**$25.95**
	"The Rev. Jean Pierre de Caussade was one of the most remarkable spiritual writers of the Society of Jesus in France in the 18th Century. His death took place at Toulouse in 1751. His works have gone through many editions and have been republished...		Inspirational/Religion Pages 400
☐	**Mental Chemistry** by *Charles Haanel*	ISBN: *1-59462-192-6*	**$23.95**
	Mental Chemistry allows the change of material conditions by combining and appropriately utilizing the power of the mind. Much like applied chemistry creates something new and unique out of careful combinations of chemicals the mastery of mental chemistry...		New Age Pages 354
☐	**The Letters of Robert Browning and Elizabeth Barret Barrett 1845-1846 vol II** by **Robert Browning** and **Elizabeth Barrett**	ISBN: *1-59462-193-4*	**$35.95**
			Biographies Pages 596
☐	**Gleanings In Genesis (volume I)** by *Arthur W. Pink*	ISBN: *1-59462-130-6*	**$27.45**
	Appropriately has Genesis been termed "the seed plot of the Bible" for in it we have, in germ form, almost all of the great doctrines which are afterwards fully developed in the books of Scripture which follow...		Religion/Inspirational Pages 420
☐	**The Master Key** by *L. W. de Laurence*	ISBN: *1-59462-001-6*	**$30.95**
	In no branch of human knowledge has there been a more lively increase of the spirit of research during the past few years than in the study of Psychology, Concentration and Mental Discipline. The requests for authentic lessons in Thought Control, Mental Discipline and...		New Age/Business Pages 422
☐	**The Lesser Key Of Solomon Goetia** by *L. W. de Laurence*	ISBN: *1-59462-092-X*	**$9.95**
	This translation of the first book of the "Lernegton" which is now for the first time made accessible to students of Talismanic Magic was done, after careful collation and edition, from numerous Ancient Manuscripts in Hebrew, Latin, and French...		New Age/Occult Pages 92
☐	**Rubaiyat Of Omar Khayyam** by *Edward Fitzgerald*	ISBN:*1-59462-332-5*	**$13.95**
	Edward Fitzgerald, whom the world has already learned, in spite of his own efforts to remain within the shadow of anonymity, to look upon as one of the rarest poets of the century, was born at Bredfield, in Suffolk, on the 31st of March, 1809. He was the third son of John Purcell...		Music Pages 172
☐	**Ancient Law** by *Henry Maine*	ISBN: *1-59462-128-4*	**$29.95**
	The chief object of the following pages is to indicate some of the earliest ideas of mankind, as they are reflected in Ancient Law, and to point out the relation of those ideas to modern thought.		Religiom/History Pages 452
☐	**Far-Away Stories** by *William J. Locke*	ISBN: *1-59462-129-2*	**$19.45**
	"Good wine needs no bush, but a collection of mixed vintages does. And this book is just such a collection. Some of the stories I do not want to remain buried for ever in the museum files of dead magazine-numbers an author's not unpardonable vanity..."		Fiction Pages 272
☐	**Life of David Crockett** by *David Crockett*	ISBN: *1-59462-250-7*	**$27.45**
	"Colonel David Crockett was one of the most remarkable men of the times in which he lived. Born in humble life, but gifted with a strong will, an indomitable courage, and unremitting perseverance...		Biographies/New Age Pages 424
☐	**Lip-Reading** by *Edward Nitchie*	ISBN: *1-59462-206-X*	**$25.95**
	Edward B. Nitchie, founder of the New York School for the Hard of Hearing, now the Nitchie School of Lip-Reading, Inc, wrote "LIP-READING Principles and Practice". The development and perfecting of this meritorious work on lip-reading was an undertaking...		How-to Pages 400
☐	**A Handbook of Suggestive Therapeutics, Applied Hypnotism, Psychic Science** by **Henry Munro**	ISBN: *1-59462-214-0*	**$24.95**
			Health/New Age/Health/Self-help Pages 376
☐	**A Doll's House: and Two Other Plays** by *Henrik Ibsen*	ISBN: *1-59462-112-8*	**$19.95**
	Henrik Ibsen created this classic when in revolutionary 1848 Rome. Introducing some striking concepts in playwriting for the realist genre, this play has been studied the world over.		Fiction/Classics/Plays 308
☐	**The Light of Asia** by *sir Edwin Arnold*	ISBN: *1-59462-204-3*	**$13.95**
	In this poetic masterpiece, Edwin Arnold describes the life and teachings of Buddha. The man who was to become known as Buddha to the world was born as Prince Gautama of India but he rejected the worldly riches and abandoned the reigns of power when...		Religion/History/Biographies Pages 170
☐	**The Complete Works of Guy de Maupassant** by *Guy de Maupassant*	ISBN: *1-59462-157-8*	**$16.95**
	"For days and days, nights and nights, I had dreamed of that first kiss which was to consecrate our engagement, and I knew not on what spot I should put my lips..."		Fiction/Classics Pages 240
☐	**The Art of Cross-Examination** by *Francis L. Wellman*	ISBN: *1-59462-309-0*	**$26.95**
	Written by a renowned trial lawyer, Wellman imparts his experience and uses case studies to explain how to use psychology to extract desired information through questioning.		How-to/Science/Reference Pages 408
☐	**Answered or Unanswered?** by *Louisa Vaughan*	ISBN: *1-59462-248-5*	**$10.95**
	Miracles of Faith in China		Religion Pages 112
☐	**The Edinburgh Lectures on Mental Science (1909)** by *Thomas*	ISBN: *1-59462-008-3*	**$11.95**
	This book contains the substance of a course of lectures recently given by the writer in the Queen Street Hall, Edinburgh. Its purpose is to indicate the Natural Principles governing the relation between Mental Action and Material Conditions...		New Age/Psychology Pages 148
☐	**Ayesha** by *H. Rider Haggard*	ISBN: *1-59462-301-5*	**$24.95**
	Verily and indeed it is the unexpected that happens! Probably if there was one person upon the earth from whom the Editor of this, and of a certain previous history, did not expect to hear again...		Classics Pages 380
☐	**Ayala's Angel** by *Anthony Trollope*	ISBN: *1-59462-352-X*	**$29.95**
	The two girls were both pretty, but Lucy who was twenty-one who supposed to be simple and comparatively unattractive, whereas Ayala was credited, as her Bombwhat romantic name might show, with poetic charm and a taste for romance. Ayala when her father died was nineteen...		Fiction Pages 484
☐	**The American Commonwealth** by *James Bryce*	ISBN: *1-59462-286-8*	**$34.45**
	An interpretation of American democratic political theory. It examines political mechanics and society from the perspective of Scotsman James Bryce		Politics Pages 572
☐	**Stories of the Pilgrims** by *Margaret P. Pumphrey*	ISBN: *1-59462-116-0*	**$17.95**
	This book explores pilgrims religious oppression in England as well as their escape to Holland and eventual crossing to America on the Mayflower, and their early days in New England...		History Pages 268

www.bookjungle.com *email: sales@bookjungle.com fax: 630-214-0564 mail: Book Jungle PO Box 2226 Champaign, IL 61825*

QTY

The Fasting Cure *by Sinclair Upton*   ISBN: *1-59462-222-1*   **$13.95**
In the Cosmopolitan Magazine for May, 1910, and in the Contemporary Review (London) for April, 1910, I published an article dealing with my experiences in fasting. I have written a great many magazine articles, but never one which attracted so much attention...   *New Age/Self Help/Health Pages 164*

Hebrew Astrology *by Sepharial*   ISBN: *1-59462-308-2*   **$13.45**
In these days of advanced thinking it is a matter of common observation that we have left many of the old landmarks behind and that we are now pressing forward to greater heights and to a wider horizon than that which represented the mind-content of our progenitors...   *Astrology Pages 144*

Thought Vibration or The Law of Attraction in the Thought World   ISBN: *1-59462-127-6*   **$12.95**
by William Walker Atkinson   *Psychology/Religion Pages 144*

Optimism *by Helen Keller*   ISBN: *1-59462-108-X*   **$15.95**
Helen Keller was blind, deaf, and mute since 19 months old, yet famously learned how to overcome these handicaps, communicate with the world, and spread her lectures promoting optimism. An inspiring read for everyone...   *Biographies/Inspirational Pages 84*

Sara Crewe *by Frances Burnett*   ISBN: *1-59462-360-0*   **$9.45**
In the first place, Miss Minchin lived in London. Her home was a large, dull, tall one, in a large, dull square, where all the houses were alike, and all the sparrows were alike, and where all the door-knockers made the same heavy sound...   *Childrens/Classic Pages 88*

The Autobiography of Benjamin Franklin *by Benjamin Franklin*   ISBN: *1-59462-135-7*   **$24.95**
The Autobiography of Benjamin Franklin has probably been more extensively read than any other American historical work, and no other book of its kind has had such ups and downs of fortune. Franklin lived for many years in England, where he was agent...   *Biographies/History Pages 332*

Name	
Email	
Telephone	
Address	
City, State ZIP	

☐ Credit Card   ☐ Check / Money Order

Credit Card Number	
Expiration Date	
Signature	

Please Mail to: Book Jungle
PO Box 2226
Champaign, IL 61825
or Fax to: 630-214-0564

ORDERING INFORMATION

web: *www.bookjungle.com*
email: *sales@bookjungle.com*
fax: *630-214-0564*
mail: *Book Jungle PO Box 2226 Champaign, IL 61825*
or PayPal *to sales@bookjungle.com*

Please contact us for bulk discounts

DIRECT-ORDER TERMS

**20% Discount if You Order
Two or More Books**
Free Domestic Shipping!
Accepted: Master Card, Visa,
Discover, American Express

www.ingramcontent.com/pod-product-compliance
Lightning Source LLC
Chambersburg PA
CBHW081350040426
42450CB00015B/3378